DREAMS IN THE SHADOWS

The Heart's Silent Struggles.

2

M. Mark Greece

Table Of Contents

ABOUT THE AUTHOR

M. Mark Greece is an acclaimed Ugandan author and editor who champions human rights through his writing. Born and raised in Uganda, Mark draws on the rich cultural heritage and challenges of his homeland to craft compelling narratives that highlight the importance of resilience and hope. His mission is to use his stories to advocate for justice and inspire positive change.

ACKNOWLEDGEME NTS

Writing "Dreams in the Shadows" has been an incredible journey filled with challenges and triumphs, and I am grateful to everyone who has supported me along the way.

First and foremost, I want to express my deepest gratitude to Opio James, whose brief but profound presence in this world inspired me to embark on this writing journey. Your memory will forever be a beacon of light in my life.

I am indebted to my family for their unwavering support and encouragement. To my friends, thank you for being my pillars of strength and for believing in me even when I doubted myself.

DEDICATION

Dedicated to Opio James, who in his brief seven years, left an indelible mark on our hearts. Your life was a lesson in the power of dreams and the strength to pursue them against all odds.

AUTHOR'S NOTE

Dear Reader,

As you embark on this journey through "Dreams in the Shadows," I want to take a moment to share with you the inspiration behind this story.

Growing up in Uganda, I witnessed firsthand the struggles and triumphs of individuals who dared to dream against all odds. "Dreams in the Shadows" is a tribute to their resilience, their spirit, and their unwavering belief in a brighter tomorrow.

Through the characters of Violet and Aiden, I hope to shine a light on the power of dreams, the strength of love, and the beauty of never giving up, no matter the challenges we face.

Thank you for joining me on this adventure. I hope this story touches your heart as much as it has touched mine.

With gratitude,

M. Mark Greece

INTRODUCTION

In the heart of rural Uganda, Violet dreams of escaping her impoverished life and becoming a football star for Manchester United. Despite societal and familial pressures to abandon her ambitions, she persists with unwavering determination. Her journey intersects with Aiden, the son of a powerful but corrupt government official. Their love story unfolds against the backdrop of political intrigue and personal sacrifice, culminating in a dramatic and heartbreaking conclusion that reveals the true cost of pursuing one's dreams.

CHAPTER 1

Rising Tension

The night was dark and stormy as Violet came into the world, a tiny beacon of hope amidst the chaos of a rioting crowd. Her mother, in the throes of labor, was being rushed to the nearest medical facility by her father. But their journey was fraught with danger, as the streets were filled with angry protestors clashing with a mob of very arrogant government forces, over the skyrocketing taxes on fuel and gas.

As they neared the outskirts of the city, the situation escalated. Shots rang out, and suddenly, Violet's father, caught in the crossfire, was fatally wounded. With his last breath, her mother Roswell urged him to continue to the medical facility, knowing that her own life, and the life of her unborn child were in grave danger.

Despite the chaos around them, they pressed on, navigating

through the crowded streets and evading the violence as best as they could. Finally, they reached the small, dimly lit room where the poor little thing would be born, with only a flickering candle to light the way.

Violet's arrival was attended by an old, weather-beaten woman. Her face lined with years of hardship. She moved with a slow, deliberate grace. Her hands gentle yet firm as she guided the baby into the world. The old woman's eyes held a mixture of sadness, and resignation, as if she had seen too much suffering in her lifetime.

As the poor little pale thin thing took its first breaths, the old woman wrapped her in cold, damp rags. The only thing available to keep her warm. Despite the roughness of her surroundings, Violet's cry was strong and full of life. A testament to her strength even at such a young age. Her mother, exhausted and grieving, looked upon her newborn daughter with a mixture of sorrow and hope, knowing that her life would never be the same again.

CHAPTER 2

Early Struggles.

The years following Violet's birth were filled with hardships. Her mother had passed away shortly after giving birth, leaving her in the care of her Aunt Melissa. A stern woman embittered by life's trials, who saw Violet as a burden. She begrudgingly provided for her niece, often reminding her that she was unwanted and a constant reminder of the family tragedy.

Violet's childhood was spent in a small, runtown ghetto in Bukaasa village, bordering the East, and central Uganda. The village was marked by poverty and neglect, with children playing barefoot in the dusty streets, and families struggling to make ends meet. Despite the harsh conditions, Violet's spirit remained unbroken. She found solace in playing football, using makeshift balls made of bundled rags and practicing on the bare ground pitches with other village children.

Her aunt disapproved of her love for football, believing it to be a waste of time and energy. "You're not going to make a life out of kicking a ball", she would say, her voice dripping with disdain. "Focus on your studies and do something useful with your life." But Violet's passion for the game could not be dampened, she would sneak out early in the morning and late in the evening to play, honing her skills and dreaming of a future where she could make a name for herself as a Manchester United player.

One day, as Violet was playing with her friends, a local coach noticed her talent. Mr. David Obua, a former National-team player, and retired footballer who had returned to the village to give back to the community, saw something special in Violet. He approached her after the game, his eyes shining with excitement. "You have a gift," he told her. "With the right training, you could go far,"

Violet's heart soared at his words. She had always believed in her own potential, but hearing it from someone else gave her much more hope. Mr. Obua offered to train her, and despite her aunt's objection, she eagerly accepted. She would wake up before dawn to meet him on the field, practicing until her muscles ached, and her clothes were drenched in sweat,

As the months passed, Violet's skills improved dramatically. She became known in the village for her speed, agility, and determination on the field. But with her growing reputation, came growing resentment from her Aunt Melissa. "You're wasting your time," she would hiss whenever Violet returned home late. "No one from this village ever amounts to anything."

Despite the harsh words and the constant struggles, Violet remained undeterred. She knew that football was her ticket out of poverty, her chance to create a better life for herself and honor the memory of her parents. Every time she stepped onto the field, she felt their presence with her, guiding her towards her dream.

One evening, after an intense training session, Violet returned home to find her aunt in a rare moment of vulnerability. "Why do you keep doing this?" her aunt asked, her voice trembling with a mixture of frustration and sadness. "Why can't you just accept your place in this world?"

Violet looked at her, her eyes filled with determination. "Because I believe I can be more," she replied softly. "And I want to prove that our circumstances don't define us."

Her aunt turned away, unable to respond. For the first time, Violet saw a flicker of understanding in her eyes. It was a small victory, but it gave her the strength to keep pushing forward. She knew the road ahead would be difficult, but with each step, she grew closer to her dream of becoming the best footballer and playing for the great Manchester United women's team.

CHAPTER 3

Meeting Aiden.

Violet's life took an unexpected turn the day she met Aiden. It was a sweltering afternoon, and Violet had just finished a grueling practice session with Mr. Obua. She was on her way to a small town clinic to buy some medicine for her aunt, who had been suffering from recurring bouts of malaria.

The clinic was a modest building, with faded paint and a few benches outside. Inside, the air was cooler, and the smell of antiseptic was strong. As Violet approached the counter, she noticed a boy about her age sitting in the waiting area. He had a mischievous glint in his eyes and an air of confidence that was hard to ignore.

This boy was Aiden, son of a high-ranking government minister who preferred to keep his family out of the public eye. Aiden had come to the clinic to visit his big sister, who worked there as a junior nurse. Despite his privileged background, he was down-to-earth, and friendly, traits that quickly caught Violet's attention.

As she waited for her turn, she couldn't help but glance at Aiden. Sensing her gaze, he looked up and flashed her a charming smile. "Hi, I'm Aiden," he said, extending a hand. Are you here for someone?

Violet hesitated for a moment before shaking his hand. "I'm Violet. I'm here to get medicine for my aunt Melisa."

Aiden's expression softened. "I'm so sorry to hear that. I hope she gets better soon."

Their conversation was cut short by the nurse calling Violet's name. She quickly purchased the medicine and turned to leave, but not before, Aiden called out to her. "Hey, Violet! Maybe I'll see you around?"

Violet smiled shyly and nodded. "Maybe."

Over the next few weeks, Violet and Aiden's paths crossed more frequently. They would bump into each other at the market, and even at the football field where Violet practiced. Each encounter brought them closer, and they began to look forward to their meetings.

Despite the growing bond between them, Violet couldn't shake the feeling that their friendship was fraught with obstacles, Aiden's father Mr. Kato, a powerful and corrupt politician responsible for many of the hardships faced by the people in Bukaasa. He had amassed a fortune by exploiting government resources, and imposing unofficial taxes on small, and growing local businesses within the entire village.

Mr. Kato was vehemently opposed to any relationship between his son and a poor village girl, fearing that it would tarnish his family's reputation. He had no idea that his son Aiden, had already developed a deep affection for Violet, and was determined to defy his father's selfish wishes.

One evening, after a particularly intense practice session, Violet and Aiden met at the clinic once again. This time, Aiden seemed more serious. "Violet, there's something I need to tell you," he began, his voice tinged with urgency. "My father... He's not who he seems. He's done terrible things, I can't stand by and let him get away with."

Violet listened intently, her heart pounding. "What do you mean?"

Aiden took a deep breath. "I have evidence of his corruption. If I expose him, it could ruin him, but might also put us in danger. I don't want to drag you into this, but I can't keep it a secret from you anymore."

Violet's mint raced. She knew that standing up to Mr. Kato would be dangerous, but she couldn't ignore the injustices. "I'll stand by you, Aiden," she said firmly. "Whatever happens, we'll face it together."

Their resolve strengthened, Violet and Aiden knew that they were in for a fight for their lives. But with each other to lean on, they felt ready to take on the world.

CHAPTER 4

Hidden Agendas.

Violet's training sessions grew more intense as she prepared for the upcoming National tournament. Mr. Obua pushed her hard, knowing that this tournament could bear a ticket to a better future. Meanwhile, her bond with Aiden deepened, and they became inseparable. Yet, the shadow of Mr. Kato loomed over their burgeoning relationship.

One hot afternoon, after a long practice, Violet and Aiden found a quiet spot under a large mango tree. The village was abuzz with preparation for the annual market day, but the tree offered a serene escape from the chaos. Aiden's expression was serious as he turned to Violet. "I've been thinking about what we discussed," he said, his voice low. "My Father... he's involved in some really bad stuff. I have to stop him, but I'm worried about what might happen to you.

Violet reached out and took his hand. "We'll face it together," she assured him. "I know it's dangerous, but we can't let him keep stealing even the very least, those poor business men and women of Bukaasa."

Just then, they heard footsteps approaching. It was Aiden's sister, Grace, who had finished her shift at the clinic. She greeted them with a warm smile. I thought I might find you here," she said. "You two need to be careful. Father is getting suspicious."

Aiden nodded. We know, Grace. But we can't just sit by and do nothing."

Grace sighed. "I understand. Just promise me you'll be careful."

Meanwhile, Mr. Kato was becoming increasingly paranoid. He had noticed Aiden's frequent absences and his growing closeness with a very poor little village girl. One evening, he called Aiden into his study. The room was dimly lit, the air thick with tension. "Aiden," Mr. Kato began, his voice cold, "I've heard rumors about you spending time with a small village girl. You know how big our family is in this entire village, and the fact that we cannot afford such distractions."

Aiden met his father's gaze, defiance burning in his eyes. "Violet is more than just a village girl," he replied. She's talented, intelligent, and deserves a chance to make something out of her life.

Mr. Kato's expression darkened. "You are not to see her again. Focus on your studies and your own future. Do you understand?"

Aiden clenched his fists, struggling to contain his anger. "I won't stop seeing her, father. And I won't stand by, while you destroy this beautiful country, that is mothering hundreds and thousands of short-tall citizens, suffering and crying because of your selfish evil dealings.

Mr. Kato's eyes narrowed. "What are you talking about?"

Aiden took a deep breath. "I know about your corruption. I've seen the documents. If you don't stop, I'll expose you."

Mr. Kato's face twisted with rage. "You ungrateful boy! You think you can threaten me? I will ruin that girl's life, and anyone who stands with her."

With that, Aiden stormed out of the study, his heart pounding. He knew the risks, but he couldn't let his father continue with his reign of terror.

The next day, Violet received a letter from Aiden. They had to be cautious and meet in secret from now on. Their love for each other gave them strength, but the danger was real and growing.

That evening, under the cover of darkness, they met near their usual old mango tree. Aiden's face was tense with worry. "My

Father is onto us," he said. "We need to be extra careful."

Violet needed her heart aching with the weight of their situation. "I know, Aiden. But we'll get through this. Together."

As they embraced the reality of their fight against Mr. Kato's, and many other government officials' corruption, their struggle for love became ever-clear. They were up against very powerful faces, but their determination and love gave them hope.

CHAPTER 5

Struggles And Strides

The National Youths' Tournament was drawing nearer, and Violet could feel the pressure mounting. Every practice session seemed to pass in a blur of sweat, pain and determination. Mr. Obua pushed her harder than ever, his stern face barely canceling his pride in her progress. "It's true you have a gift, Violet," he would say, "but gifts are nothing without hard work."

One evening, as the sun dipped below the horizon, casting the village in a warm, golden glow, Violet received an urgent message from Aiden. They were to meet at their usual spot by the old mango tree. Her heart pounded with a mixture of excitement and dread that something was wrong.

When she arrived, Aiden was already there, pacing like a caged lion. His eyes were wild with fear and determination. "Violet," he began, his voice trembling, "my father is planning something terrible. He's going to frame you and Mr. Obua for theft to ruin your chances in the upcoming tournament."

Violet felt a cold chill run down her spine. "Why would he do that?"

Aiden's jaw tightened. "To keep us apart, and to send a message that no one crosses him without consequences."

Violet's mind raced. The thoughts of her dream being shattered by such deceit was unbearable. "What can we do?"

Aiden stepped closer, his eyes burning with intensity. "We need to find the evidence before he can act. There's a hidden room in our house where he keeps his most important documents. If we can get there, we might find proof of his evil plans."

Violet nodded, her resolve hardening. "Let's do it my dear."

The plan was fraught with danger. Sneaking into Mr. Kato household undetected would be nearly impossible, but they had no other choice. That night, as shadows danced under the pale moonlight, they made their move.

Violet felt her heart hammering in the chest as they crept through the back streets. The mansion loomed ahead, a dark silhouette against the sky. They slipped through the garden, carefully to avoid the guards. Aiden led the way, his knowledge of their house, their only advantage.

Inside, the air was thick with tension. They moved silently, like ghosts, through the grand halls every creak of the floorboards, every distant sound, felt like an alarm. Finally, they reached the hidden room. Aiden's hands shook as he fumbled with the lock. "Hurry up please, 'Violet whispered, her voice barely audible.

The door clicked open, revealing a room filled with shelves of documents and a large desk. They quickly began searching, the minutes ticking away like a time bomb. Suddenly, Violet's eyes landed on a folder marked "Operation Sabotage."

"This must be it," she said, pulling it from the shelf.

As they leafed through the documents, the damning evidence came to light. Plans to plant stolen goods in Mr. Obua home, forged signatures, and detailed instructions on how to frame them. It was all there.

"We need to get this to the authorities," Aiden said, his voice urgent.

But as they turned to leave, they heard footsteps approaching. Mr. Kato appeared in the doorway, his face a mask of fury. "What do you think you're doing"? He snarled.

Violet felt a surge of fear, but she stood her ground. We're not letting you get away with this."

Mr. Kato laughed, a sound devoid of humor. "You think you can stop me? You're nothing but a poor village girl and a disobedient son. You can't win."

Aiden stepped forward, his voice steady. "Maybe not, but we won't let you destroy innocent lives."

With that, they ran, clutching the folder like a lifeline. The night air was cool against their skin as they dashed through the garden, Mr. Kato's shouts echoing behind them. They had the evidence, but their fight was far from over.

As they reached the village, Violet felt a flicker of hope. They had taken the first step in exposing Mr. Kato's corruption, but the path ahead was treacherous. The tension between love, duty, and survival was sharper than ever, and the stakes had never been higher.

CHAPTER 6

Unseen Shadows

The days leading up to the tournament were filled with a mixture of hope and dread. Violet poured everything she had into her training, determined to prove herself. Yet, amid the rigorous practices and fleeting moments of joy, a shadow loomed over her.

It started with headaches, small and frequent at first. Violet brushed them off, attributing them to stress and exhaustion. But as the days passed, the pain grew more intense, like a vise tightening around her skull. She didn't tell anyone, not wanting to appear weak or risk missing the tournament. She couldn't afford a doctor's visit anyway; her aunt barely managed to keep food on the table.

One afternoon, as the sun blazed high in the sky, Violet found herself alone on the pitch, practicing her dribbling. Sweat dripped down her face, and her vision blurred momentarily. She stopped, leaning on her knees, waiting for the dizziness to pass. Aiden arrived, noticing her discomfort.

"Are you okay, Violet?" he asked, concern etching his face.

"I'm fine," she lied, forcing a smile. "Just tired."

Aiden didn't press further, but worry gnawed at him. He had seen her struggle more frequently, her energy waning. Still, she pushed on, her spirit unyielding.

Later that evening, they met at a secret spot by the river. The cool breeze was a welcome relief from the day's heat. They sat close to each other, watching the water ripple under the moonlight.

"Violet, you know you can tell me anything, right?" Aiden said softly, taking her hand in his.

She looked at him, her eyes reflecting the moon's glow. "I know Aiden. It's just… everything feels so heavy. The tournament, Mr. Kato, my aunt. It's a lot."

Aiden squeezed her hand gently. "We'll get through it together."

Days turned into weeks, and the tournament loomed closer. Violet's symptoms worsened. She began to lose her balance occasionally, her headaches becoming unbearable. But she kept it hidden, afraid of what the truth might mean.

Then came the night everything changed.

It was late, and Violet had just finished a grueling practice. She was walking home when she felt a sharp, blinding pain in her head. She stumbled, barely catching herself on a nearby fence. The world spun around her, and she fell to her knees.

Aiden, who had been following her from a distance, rushed to her side. "Violet! What's happening?"

She looked up at him, tears streaming down her face. "I don't know, Aiden, it hurts so much."

He helped her to her feet, his heart pounding with fear. "We need to get you a doctor."

"No," she protested weakly. "I can't afford it, and the tournament…"

"Forget the tournament," Aiden snapped. "Your health is more important."

Reluctantly, Violet agreed. They went to the small clinic where Aiden's sister worked as a junior nurse. She was shocked to see Violet in such a state and immediately began to examine her.

"We need to run some tests," she said, her face grim. "This could be serious."

As they waited for the results, Aiden held Violet's hand, his mind racing. The thought of losing her was unbearable. He couldn't shake the feeling that his father's schemes and the stress they had caused had contributed to her condition.

Finally, the nurse returned, her expression somber. "Violet, we need to talk. The tests indicate signs of a brain tumor."

The room fell silent. Violet felt as if the ground had been ripped from beneath her. Aiden's grip tightened, his eyes wide with shock.

"A tumor?" Violet whispered, her voice barely audible.

The nurse nodded. "Yes. We need to do more tests to be certain, but it's critical that you see a specialist."

Aiden turned to her, his voice filled with determination. "We'll get through this, Violet. I promise."

Violet nodded, tears filling her eyes. The weight of her dreams, her struggles, and now her illness pressed heavily on her. Yet, even in this darkest moment, she felt a flicker of hope. She wasn't alone. Aiden was with her, and together, they would face whatever came next.

The revelation of Violet's illness added a new layer of urgency and tension to their fight against Mr. Kato. It was no longer just about dreams and love; it was about survival, and the stakes had never been higher.

CHAPTER 7

The Ultimatum

The revelation of Violet's illness weighed heavily on her, but she resolved to keep it a secret from everyone except Aiden and his sister. She didn't want to burden her friends and teammates with her struggles, especially with the tournament so close. Every morning, she woke with a renewed determination to push through the pain and give her all on the field.

Meanwhile, Mr. Kato was not idle. Furious at his son's defiance and the bond he had formed with Violet, he devised a new plan. Knowing that Violet's Aunt Melisa harbored no love for her niece, and was always looking for an escape route from poverty, in case she saw any opportunity.

One evening, Mr. Kato paid a visit to Melissa's humble home. The sound of his expensive brand new Ford-mustang drew curious glances from the villagers of Bukaasa. Melisa greeted him with a mix of suspicion and hope. She invited him inside, where the dim light of an old kerosene lamp cast long shadows on the walls.

Mr. Kato wasted no time. "Melisa, I have a proposition for you. I know life here is hard, and you're struggling to make ends meet. What if I told you I could offer you a way out" a fresh start, far from Bukaasa village."

Melisa's eyes narrowed. "What do you mean?"

"I can provide you with enough money to leave this place and start a new life. All you need to do is take that so-called Violet thing with you, and ensure it never returns.

Melisa's heart raced. The prospect of leaving the village where she had spent her entire life, the poverty, and the endless struggles was tempting. "And what do you get out of this?"

Mr. Kato's smile was cold. "Let's just say it's in my best interest that your little demon is no longer a destruction for my only son."

Melisa considered the offer. It was a chance to escape, something she had longed for. But it meant uprooting Violet, taking her away from her dreams and friends, yet, the lure of a better life was strong. "Alright I'll do it."

Satisfied, Mr. Kato handed her a large sum of cash. "You need to leave as soon as possible. Tell Violet it's for her own good."

That night, Melissa approached Violet. She found her sitting outside, looking at the stars. "Violet, we need to talk."

Violet looked up, surprised by the seriousness in her aunt's tone. "What is it, Aunt Melissa?"

We're leaving the village. I've found a way for us to have a better life, far from Bukaasa."

Violet's heart sank. "But the tournament... my friends... Aiden..."

Melissa's face hardened. "Forget the tournament my dear. This is about your future. You'll have a chance to live a comfortable life, away from the struggles and pains of this place."

But aunt, I can't just leave. You know that football is everything to me. My coach Mr. Obua... and Aiden... they've helped me so much."

Melissa sighed, her patience waning. This isn't up for discussion, Violet. We're leaving and that's final."

Desperation welled up inside Violet. She couldn't abandon everything she had worked for, not when she was so close to achieving her dream. "I can't go, aunt. I belong here."

Melisa's eyes flashed with anger, "you ungrateful child! Do you think staying here playing football will change anything? This is your chance to escape poverty, and live a better life!"

Violet stood her ground. My life is here, with my friends, my team, my coach Mr. Obua, and Aiden. I won't go."

Melissa's frustration reached its peak. "Fine. Stay here and waste your life away. But don't ever come crying to me, when reality crushes all your dreams."

With that, Melissa stormed off, leaving Violet alone with her thoughts. The weight of the decision pressed down on her, but she couldn't abandon her dreams. Not now, not ever.

The following days were filled with a tense silence between Violet and her Aunt Melisa, who had packed all her belongings, preparing to leave the village alone. Violet continued to train pushing through the pain of her illness and the emotional turmoil caused by her aunt's betrayal.

As the tournament approached, Violet's resolve hardened. She knew the path ahead would be difficult, but she had Aiden by her side, and together they would face whatever challenges came their way.

CHAPTER 8

The Tournament.

The day of the tournament arrived with a mix of excitement and tension. The entire village turned out to support their team, hoping for a victory that would bring them pride and joy. The atmosphere in the stadium was so electric, with banners waving and chants echoing through the air. Violet, despite her secret illness, felt a surge of determination. She knew this was her moment to shine, to prove to everyone that her dreams were worth fighting for.

As the match began, Violet's team faced fierce competition. The opposing team was so strong and well-coordinated, but Violet's skills and leadership kept her team in the game. She moved across the field with grace and agility, her focus unwavering despite the occasional pangs of pain she felt in her head. Her coach Mr. Obua, a grizzled old man who had seen her potential from the start, stood on the sidelines, cheering her on with every move she made. He shouted words of encouragement, his voice hoarse but filled with pride.

The game was intense, with both teams scoring and defending with equal favor. Violet faced numerous tackles from the opposing players, their aggression leaving her feet bruised and bleeding. Her old torn boots offered little protection, and with every step, she felt the sting of pain. But she refused to give up, pushing through the agony with sheer willpower. Aiden, watching from the sidelines, felt a mixture of pride and worry. He knew about Violet's secret condition, and feared for her health, but he also admired her unbreakable spirit.

In the dying minutes of the game, the tension in the stadium reached its peak. The opposing team launched a powerful strike that seemed destined for the back of the net. The crowd held their breath as their goalkeeper dived, missing the ball completely. But by a stroke of luck, the ball struck the bar of the net and ricocheted back into play. The rebound fell to Violet, who seized the opportunity for a counter-attack. With remarkable speed and skill, Violet sprinted down the field, dodging the defenders left and right. She weaved through various opponents, her movements a blur of determination and fineness. Her teammates watched in awe as she single-handedly drove the ball towards their opponent's goal. The stadium was silent, the crowd collectively holding their heads and breath.

As Violet approached the goal, the opposing goalkeeper advanced, trying to cut off her angle, with her hands spread apart. With a swift and powerful kick, Violet sent the ball soaring through the air. It curved perfectly, sailing past the outstretched hands of the goalkeeper and into the net. The crowd erupted in cheers, celebrating the wonder goal that had secured their victory.

Violet, overwhelmed with joy, threw her hands into the air and began celebrating wildly. Her teammates rushed to her, tackling her in a joyful heap. They piled on top of her. Laughter and cheers filling the air. Violet's smile was radiant, her face glowing with the triumph she had worked so hard for. It was a moment of pure, unadulterated happiness.

But as the celebration continued, something felt wrong. After a few moments, Violet's teammates noticed her lack of response. The cheers turned into murmurs of concern, as they quickly tried to check on her. Her eyes were closed, her body unnaturally still. Panic set in as they realized she wasn't moving.

"Aiden! Aiden!" one of the players shouted, looking towards the sidelines. Aiden, who had been cheering, froze as he saw the commotion. His heart raced as he sprinted onto the field, stumbling and falling in his haste to reach Violet. His panic was evident, his fear palpable.

"Violet, wake up!" Aiden pleaded, kneeling beside her. He shook her gently, his voice breaking. "Somebody get help! Now!"

The medical team rushed onto the field, pushing through the concerned players. They quickly assessed the situation, and lifted her onto a stretcher. Aiden followed closely, his heart pounding with fear and desperation. He tripled several times, his leg weak with panic, but he refused to leave her side.

At the hospital, doctors and nurses worked frantically to stabilize Violet. Her condition was critical, and they quickly realized that the cause was more severe than they had initially thought. Word of Violet's condition spread quickly, and the entire village had gathered outside the hospital, waiting anxiously for the news.

Meanwhile, one of Mr. Kato's informants, who had been keeping an eye on the situation immediately reported to him. Mr. Kato, upon hearing the news, felt a twist of sense of satisfaction. He had hoped to remove Violet from his son's life, which he had somewhere somehow failed too, but then fate seemed to have done the job for him.

Inside the hospital, Aiden stayed by Violet's side, holding her hand and praying for her recovery. But despite the doctor's efforts, it was clear that Violet's condition was deteriorating. Her brain cancer, which had remained hidden for so long, was now taking its toll.

Hours passed, and the tension outside the hospital grew. Finally, a doctor emerged, his face grim. He addressed the crowd, his voice heavy with sorrow. "I'm afraid we have some bad news. Violet's condition is critical, and we're doing everything we can. Please keep her in your thoughts and prayers."

The news hit the village hard. Violet had been their beacon of hope, and now she was fighting for her life.

Later in the night, as the village waited anxiously, a new wave of horror struck. A fire had broken out at Melissa's new bar, which had been located in Katuma, where she had fled to start afresh. The bar, a modest wooden structure adorned with simple decorations, was nestled along the busy dusty street of the village's heart.. The location had promised a new beginning, far from that of Bukaasa, and the memories of struggle.

The flames spread rapidly, fueled by the wooden structure and the alcohol inside. Despite the villagers' best efforts, the fire could not be contained, and within no time, the building was reduced to ashes. The once hopeful ambiance of the bar was now a smoldering ruin, its promise of a new life for Violet's aunt Melissa had instead set her ablaze, bringing her life to an end.

In the chaos, rumors began to spread that the fire had been deliberately set. Whispers of a planned fatal accident circulated, casting a shadow of suspicion over Mr. Kato. Many believed that he had orchestrated the fire to ensure that Violet would never recover, removing any threat to his plans for Aiden.

The next morning, the village awoke to the devastating news that Violet had passed away during the night. Her death left a void that would be felt for years to come. The tournament victory, which should have been a moment of celebration, was now overshadowed by grief and loss.

Aiden, heartbroken and filled with anger, vowed to honor Violet's memory. He knew that exposing his father's corruption and ensuring justice for Violet was the only way to find peace. The journey ahead would be difficult, but with Violet's spirit guiding him, he left ready to face whatever challenges lay ahead.

CHAPTER 9

Unraveling The Truth

The village was plunged into mourning after Violet's death. Her vibrant spirit, which had inspired so many, was now a memory that brought both pain and pride. Aiden was divested but resolute. He knew he had to honor Violet by revealing the truth about his father and ensuring justice for her.

Aiden spent days gathering evidence against Mr. Kato. He sifted through documents, spoke to people who had been wronged, and pieced together the puzzle of his father's corrupt activities. He discovered how Mr. Kato had used his government position to siphon funds meant for public services, including the medical sector. The one that should have gone to improve hospitals and clinics had instead lined his father's pockets, leaving the healthcare system in shambles.

The more Aiden uncovered, the more he realized the depth of his father's betrayal. Mr. Kato's wealth had been built on the suffering of the poor, including Violet, her Aunt Melissa, and many other poor helpless families. Aiden's anger grew as he understood the extent of his father's greed and callousness. He knew he had to act, but the risk was enormous. Exposing Mr. Kato could put his own life in danger.

One evening, Aiden confronted his father in their lavish home. The contrast between the opulence of their surroundings and the poverty of the village fueled his determination. "Father, I know what you've been doing," Aiden said, his voice steady despite his anger. "I've seen the documents, spoken to people, you've been stealing from. The very people you're supposed to help."

Mr. Kato's eyes narrowed. "You don't understand the complexities of politics, Aiden. Sometimes sacrifices have to be made for the greater good."

"Don't give me that," Aiden retorted. "This isn't about politics. This is about greed and corruption. You've destroyed lives, including Violet's and her Aunt Melissa. How can you live with yourself?"

Mr. Kato's face hardened. "You think you can threaten me? Do you know what will happen if you go public with this? You'll destroy yourself along with me."

"I don't care," Aiden replied. "I'm willing to risk everything to see justice done. Violet and her aunt's death won't be in vain."

Mr. Kato's demeanor shifted from anger to desperation. "Aiden, listen to me. I can't make this go away. We can find a way to fix this without tearing our family apart. Just let it go."

Aiden shook his head. "No, father. This ends now. I'm going to the authorities, and you're going to face the consequences of your actions."

As Aiden turned to leave, Mr. Kato lunged at him, grabbing his arm. "You won't make it that far," he hissed. "I'll do whatever it takes to protect myself."

Aiden wrenched his arm free and walked out of the room, his heart pounding. He knew his father was dangerous, but he was determined to see this through. He contacted a trusted journalist and provided the evidence he had gathered, knowing that public exposure was the only way to ensure his fathers' downfall.

In the days that followed, the village buzzed with news of the scandal. Headlines blared Mr. Kato's corruption, and investigations were launched. The villagers, once afraid to speak out, inspired them to stand up for what was right.

As the investigations progressed, Mr. Kato's desperate attempts to silence his son grew more intense. He hired thugs to intimidate

Aiden, but Aiden's resolve never wavered. He found solace in the support of the villagers, who had once looked up to Mr. Kato, but now saw him for what he truly was.

One evening, Aiden received a message from an anonymous source, warning him that his life was in imminent danger. He realized that his father would stop at nothing to protect himself. Aiden knew he had to leave the village temporarily to stay safe. He packed a small bag and slipped away under the cover of the night, his heart heavy with the acknowledgement that he might never return.

Despite the danger, Aiden continued to communicate with the journalist, providing updates and new evidence. The journalist's articles painted a vivid picture of Mr. Kato's corrupt dealings, and public outrage grew. Protests erupted, demanding justice for Violet, her poor Aunt Melissa, and all others who had suffered because of Mr. Kato's greed.

Aiden's determination led him to reveal even more about his family's dark secrets. He leaked information about his mother's death, which had been shrouded in mystery. As a little boy, Aiden had witnessed his mother's opposition to his father's evil deeds. She had discovered her husband's secret affair with his closest friend's 17 year old only daughter, and her mother. Her discovery and defiance sealed her fate. The revelation added fuel to the fire, showing the extent of Mr. Kato's ruthlessness and immorality.

In a final act of desperation, Mr. Kato arranged a press conference, hoping to salvage his reputation. He stood before the cameras, his demeanor calm but his eyes betraying his fear. "I am deeply saddened by the allegations against me," he began. "But I assure you, I have always acted in the best interest of our community."

As he spoke, Aiden, hidden in the crowd, watched with a mix of anger and determination. He knew this was the moment to reveal the ultimate truth. When Mr. Kato finished his speech, Aiden stepped forward, holding a file of damning evidence.

"Lies will no longer protect you, father," Aiden said, his voice clear and unwavering. "The truth will."

The crowd gasped as Aiden handed the file to the journalist, who immediately began reading the contents aloud. The evidence was irrefutable, Mr. Kato façade crumbled. The press conference erupted into chaos as reporters bombarded Mr. Kato with questions, and the villagers cheered for Aiden's bravery.

In the aftermath, Mr. Kato was arrested and charged with numerous counts of corruption and embezzlement. Aiden returned to the village, where he was welcomed as a hero. He had risked everything to honor Violet's memory and bring justice to his community.

As the village began to heal, Aiden reflected on the journey that had brought him here. Violet's dream of becoming a football star had been cut short, but her legacy lived on in the hearts of those she had inspired. Aiden knew that he would continue to fight for a better future, one where dreams could flourish and justice would prevail...

CHAPTER 10

The Final Whistle.

The village was abuzz with anticipation. The memorial match to honor Violet's memory and raise funds for a new community health center had drawn attention from far and wide. The stadium was packed, not just with villagers, but with journalists and supporters who had been moved by Violet's story. The atmosphere was electric, charged with a mic of sorrow and pride.

Aiden stood on the pitch, gripping the ball tightly. Every corner of the stadium was filled with faces reflecting the impact Violet had made. He took a deep breath, feeling the weight of her dreams and the community's hope on his shoulders. The ball in his hands was the same one Violet had used to score her final unforgettable goal. A symbol of her indomitable spirit.

The whistle blew, and the game began. Each play, each pass, and every tackle carried the energy of a community united by Violet's legacy. Aiden played with fierce determination, every move a tribute to Violet. The crowd's cheers and gasps echoed around the stadium, a chorus of support and remembrance.

As the match progressed, the score remained tied. In the final minutes, Aiden found himself in possession of the ball. The stadium held its breath as he charged towards the goal. With a burst of speed and a powerful kick, he sent the ball flying. It soared through the air, time seeming too slow, before it struck the back of the net.

The crowd erupted in jubilation, their cheers a thunderous wave of sound. Aiden fell to his knees, tears streaming down his face as his teammates, and Mr. Obua surrounded him in a jubilant embrace. He looked up at the sky, silently dedicating the moment to Violet. He could almost feel her presence, her spirit alive in every cheer and every heart that had been touched by her story.

After the match, a ceremony was held to dedicate the new health center in Violet's name. Aiden stood at the podium, his voice steady despite the emotion threatening to overwhelm him. "Violet was more than a footballer." He began. "She was a symbol of hope, of what it means to dream against all odds. This health center stands as a testament to her legacy, a place where our community can come together to heal and thrive.

The villagers listened, their eyes filled with tears and resolve. They had learned the importance of unity, of supporting one another in times of hardships. Violet's journey had shown them that even in the darkest moment, dreams could light the way to a better future.

In the months that followed, the village transformed. The health center became a beacon of hope, funded by donations from those inspired by Violet's story. Sports programs were established to nurture young talent, ensuring that no child's dream would be dismissed. The community, once divided by struggle, found strength in their collective spirit, driven by the lessons learned from Violet's life.

Aiden shared a poignant detail from Violet's final moment. She had whispered her wish for the village to unite, to build a future where no child had to choose between their dreams and survival. It was a wish that resonated deeply, and Aiden vowed to make it a reality.

A Dream Lives On

One evening, as the sun set over the dark soils of Bukaasa village, casting a warm glow over the fields and homes, Aiden stood at the edge of the memorial football pitch. He watched a group of girls of similar age playing with joy and pride. Among them was a small little girl with a fierce determination in her eyes. So reminiscent of Violet. Aiden smiled, knowing that Violet's dream lived on in every kick, every cheer, and every heart inspired by her story.

The final moments of Violet's life had left a profound impact during the memorial match, Aiden played with everything he had, pushing through the pain and exhaustion. As he scored the winning goal, he felt a surge of emotion, a mixture of triumph and loss. The celebration that followed was bittersweet, with tears and cheers blending into a single, powerful expression of the village's love for Violet.

In the end, Violet's legacy was one of hope, resilience, and unity. Her story had shown the village-and the world-that even in the face of insurmountable odds, dreams could inspire and bring about change. The health center, the sports programs, and the community's newfound strength all stood as testaments to the power of one girl's unwavering spirit.

As Aiden looked out at the setting sun, he knew that Violet's story was far from over. It lived on in the hearts of those she had touched, a reminder that dreams, on matter how impossible they seemed, could light the way to a brighter future. And in that moment, he left a sense of peace, knowing that Violet's dream had not only changed his life but had also united a community and inspired a world.

The final whistle had blown, but the game of life continued. In every heart that had been touched by Violet's spirit, her dream lived on, a testament to the enduring power of hope, love, and unity.

THE END...

DISCLAIMER

This is a work of fiction. Names, characters, places, and incidents are either the product of the author's imagination or used fictitiously. Any resemblance to actual persons, living or dead, events, or locales is entirely coincidental.

The views and opinions expressed in this novel are those of the characters and do not necessarily reflect the official policy or position of any agency, organization, employer, or company. The author has taken care to ensure that all information is accurate and up-to-date at the time of publication; however, the author assumes no responsibility for errors or omissions, or for any consequences arising from the use of the information contained in this book.

The author reserves the right to change, alter, or modify any part of this novel at their discretion and without prior notice. This novel is intended for entertainment purposes only and should not be used as a source of factual information.

APPENDIX

Political And Social Context Of Uganda

Historical Background

Uganda, often referred to as the "Pearl of Africa," is a country rich in cultural diversity and natural beauty. However, its history has been marked by periods of political instability, conflict, and economic challenges. Understanding this context is crucial to appreciating the backdrop against which Violet's story unfolds.

°**Colonial Era**: Uganda was a British colony from 1894 until it gained independence in 1962. The colonial period saw the establishment of modern infrastructure but also laid the groundwork for ethnic divisions and economic disparities.

° **Post-Independence Era**: Following independence, Uganda experienced a series of turbulent political changes, including military coups and dictatorial regimes. The most notorious period was under Idi Amin (1971-1979), characterized by widespread human rights abuses and economic decline.

°**Contemporary Uganda:** Today, Uganda is a republic with a multi-party political system. Despite relative stability in recent years, the country faces ongoing challenges, including political corruption, poverty, and limited access to education and healthcare.

Cultural Landscape

°**Ethnic Diversity:** Uganda is home to a wide array of ethnic groups, each with its own language, traditions, and customs. This diversity enriches the cultural tapestry of the nation but can also be a source of tension.

°**Traditional Practices:** Many Ugandans maintain strong ties to traditional practices and beliefs, which play a significant role in community life and identity.

°**Sports and Entertainment:** Football is the most popular sport in Uganda, providing a sense of unity and pride among its people. It serves as a critical outlet for youth, offering opportunities for personal development and social mobility.

Economic Challenges

° **Poverty**: A significant portion of Uganda's population lives below the poverty line, with limited access to basic services such as clean water, healthcare, and education.

° **Employment**: Unemployment rates are high, particularly among the youth. Many young people turn to informal sectors for work, which are often precarious and poorly paid

°**Agriculture**: The economy is primarily agricultural, with the majority of the population engaged in subsistence farming. This reliance on agriculture makes the country vulnerable to climate change and global market fluctuations.

Key Locations In The Novel

°**Violet's Village (Bukaasa)**: A small, rural community where Violet grows up. It is characterized by its close-knit community and traditional lifestyle.

°**The City (Katuma)**: Represents the broader socio-economic challenges and opportunities in Uganda, where Violet and her family face numerous struggles and conflicts.

°**Football Pitch**: A symbol of hope and aspiration, where Violet hones her skills and dreams of a better future.

Important Characters.

°**Violet**: The protagonist, a young girl with a passion for football and dreams of playing for Manchester United

°**Aiden**: Violet's love interest, who comes from a privileged background but shares her passion for football.

°**Mr. Kato**: A powerful figure who represents the oppressive forces that Violet and Aiden must confront.

°**Violet's Mother**: A symbol of strength and resilience, whose tragic death profoundly impacts Violet's life.

°   **Violet's Aunt Melissa**: A complex character who provides for Violet but also faces her own struggles and moral dilemmas.

HISTORICAL TIMELINE

Pre-Colonial Era

° **Before 1894**: Uganda is a region inhabited by various ethnic groups with rich cultures and traditions. Prominent kingdoms include Buganda, Bunyoro, Toro, and Ankole.

Colonial Period

°**1894**: Uganda becomes a British protectorate, leading to significant changes in political, social, and economic structures.

°**1945-1960**: A period of increasing resistance against colonial rule, with political parties and movements advocating for independence.

Post-Independence

°**1962**: Uganda gains independence from Britain. Milton Obote becomes the first Prime Minister.

°**1971**: Idi Amin seizes power in a military coup, leading to a brutal regime marked by human rights abuses and economic decline.

°**1979**: Idi Amin's regime is overthrown with the help of Tanzanian forces and Ugandan exiles.

°**1980**: Milton Obote returns to power, leading to continued political instability and conflict.

°**1986**: Yoweri Kaguta Museveni Tibuhabura and the National Resistance Army (NRA) take power after a protracted guerrilla war, bringing some stability but also leading to long-term challenges.

Modern Era

°**1990s**: Uganda experiences economic reforms and recovery but continues to face political challenges and human rights issues.

°**2000s**: Increased efforts to combat HIV/AIDS and promote economic development, though political tensions remain.

Setting Of "Dreams In The Shadows"

Present Day: The novel is set in contemporary Uganda, amidst ongoing social and economic challenges. The backdrop includes protests against government policies, such as the imposition of high taxes on fuel and gas, reflecting ongoing public dissatisfaction and calls for reform.

Important Events In The Novel

Early Life of Violet.

°**Birth**: Violet is born during a night of intense protests and clashes over rising fuel and gas taxes.

° **Childhood**: Violet's early years are marked by hardship, with her mother passing away and her being raised by her aunt in a poor village.

Football Journey

°**Discovery of Talent**: Violet discovers her passion and talent for football, practicing on bare ground with old, torn boots.

°**Rising Star**: Despite societal and familial challenges, Violet becomes a local football hero, inspiring others with her dedication and skill.

Climax and Tragedy

° **Tournament**: Violet's talent shines at a crucial football tournament, where she scores a spectacular goal.

° **Revelation of Illness**: During the celebration, Violet collapses, and it is revealed that she has been suffering from brain cancer.

° **Death**: Violet's passing shocks the community and prompts reflection on her life and legacy.

AFTERMATH

°**Impact**: Violet's story leaves a lasting impact on those who knew her, highlighting the themes of resilience, hope, and the pursuit of dreams despite overwhelming odds.

M. MARK GREECE